COVER: ISLE OF LEWIS PIPER; GRUINARD BAY, WESTER ROSS

Written by John Brooks

Look at Scotland

JARROLD COLOUR PUBLICATIONS

MELROSE ABBEY

SCOTT'S VIEW

The spirit of romance has always lingered in Scotland, nurtured by its grand, awesome scenery, its turbulent history, and by the vivid imagination of its people. In the early nineteenth century this highly charged atmosphere was portrayed by the masterly pen of Sir Walter Scott, the doyen of all romantic novelists as well as being a great writer of verse, who took the great events of history as a basis for stories of chivalry, adventure, and courtly love. His fame is reflected in the fact that the wide area of the Borders Region in the south of the country is now known as the Scott Country. This is centred on the great monastic centres of Melrose and Dryburgh (Scott is buried among the tree-shaded ruins of the latter abbey). From his home at Abbotsford, near Melrose, he used to drive out to a viewpoint overlooking the River Tweed, with the Eildon Hills beyond, now known as Scott's View. Southern Scotland is too often neglected as tourists make a breathless dash towards the more spectacular beauties of the Highlands. Those that pause to linger among its delightful market-towns and softly folded hills will discover beauty-spots like St Mary's Loch, hidden in the lonely countryside between Selkirk and Moffat, and famous for its literary connections with James Hogg (the Ettrick Shepherd), Scott and Wordsworth. The latter wrote an elegiac poem on its beauty called *Yarrow Visited*, while Scott used it as a setting for his epic *Marmion*.

ST MARY'S LOCH

Sir Walter Scott a vécu et travaillé près de Melrose, dans la région qui borde l'Angleterre. C'est une belle région riche en souvenirs littéraires et historiques. Les ruines de l'abbaye de Melrose sont parmi les plus beaux monuments médiévaux d'Ecosse.

Sir Walter Scott lebte nahe Melrose im südschottischen Grenzland. Dies ist eine Landschaft mit sanften Hugeln und einem reichen literarischen und historischen Erbe. Melrose Abbey ist eines der schönsten mittelalterlichen Gebäude in Schottland.

◄ ABBOTSFORD HOUSE,

PORT WILLIAM, GALLOWAY
SCAUR WATER, NEAR THORNHILL, DUMFRIES AND GALLOWAY

Sir Walter Scott was beset by financial difficulties for much of his life and this, in part, accounted for his prolific output. He built his beloved Abbotsford House on the banks of the Tweed outside Melrose; a fairy-tale house of towers and turrets where he died in 1832. Abbotsford is an interesting venue for visitors to the Borders who can see here many relics of the great writer, the rooms being furnished as they were in his day. Many of the trees in the surrounding park were planted by Scott himself. To the west of the Scott Country lies the ancient market-town of Dumfries, rich in associations with another great Scottish poet, Robert Burns. The surrounding countryside has a distinctive charm of its own — the great salmon rivers, the Annan, Nith and Cree, being fed by sparkling streams tumbling from the hills. Scaur Water is just one of these; it flows close to the great palace of the Dukes of Buccleuch, Drumlanrig Castle, now open to the public. It dates from 1676 and was occupied by Bonnie Prince Charlie during the course of his great southward march of 1745. The nearest town is Thornhill. Galloway is the district in the extreme south-west corner of Scotland. Its pleasing mixture of fine inland and coastal scenery is popular with holidaymakers who enjoy staying at peaceful little resorts like Port William, founded by Sir William Maxwell in 1770. Further to the west on the inlet known as Loch Ryan is Stranraer, important for its rail-sea link with Ulster.

Abbotsford House, près de Melrose, fut construite par Sir Walter Scott qui y mourut en 1832. Les visiteurs de la maison peuvent y voir de nombreux souvenirs du grand écrivain. La région de Dumfries et Galloway occupe l'extrémité sud-ouest de l'Ecosse.

Abbotsford House, nahe Melrose, wurde von Sir Walter Scott gebaut, der dort im Jahre 1832 starb. Viele Gegenstände in dem Haus erinnern an den Schriftsteller Der Bezirk von Dumfries und Galloway unfaßt den südwestlichen Zipfel Schottlands.

CARLINGWARK LOCH, CASTLE DOUGLAS, DUMFRIES AND GALLOWAY

GIRVAN, STRATHCLYDE

Castle Douglas is a pleasing town on the main Dumfries to Stranraer trunk road. It is situated on the shore of Carlingwark Loch, picturesquely fringed with beech trees which are splendidly colourful in the autumn when their leaves turn golden. The town only came into existence in 1792 when the village of Carlingwark changed its name to honour its landowner, Sir William Douglas of Gelston. Castle Douglas has steadily increased in importance, finally outstripping the ancient county town of Kirkcudbright ten miles to the south-west. Girvan is a busy fishing port on the Firth of Clyde coast. Offshore is the islet of Ailsa Craig, 1,114 feet high and occupied only by sea-birds, though its granite quarries are occasionally worked to provide curling-stones. It can be seen from much of the road that follows the coast northwards from Stranraer. The scenery inland is well worth exploring, especially that contained within the Glen Trool National Park. To the north of Girvan is the ancient town of Ayr which is also a fishing port but is most famous for its connections with the tempestuous life of Robert Burns. The great poet was born in 1759 in a humble cottage in the village of Alloway just to the south of the town. The cottage is open to visitors. The Burns Monument, also at Alloway, overlooks the 'Auld Brig' that spans the River Doon. The 'Burns Country' is centred on the town of Ayr, though the golf courses close by at Prestwick and Troon add to its fame.

ROBERT BURNS'S BIRTHPLACE, ALLOWAY, STRATHCLYDE

La ville d'Ayr, dans la région de Strathclyde au sud de l'Ecosse, est le centre du pays d'origine du poète Robert Burns. Le grand poète est né dans une humble chaumière à Alloway, tout près de cette ville, et on peut y voir de nombreux souvenirs dignes d'intérêt.

Das „Burns Country" umgibt die Stadt Ayr im Strathclyde-Bezirk von Südschottland. Der große Dichter wurde eben außerhalb der Stadt in einer ärmlichen Hütte in Alloway geboren, wo viele interessante Erinnerungsstücke zu besichtigen sind.

The region of Strathclyde embraces a wide area of central Scotland, from the resorts of the Firth of Clyde coast to the south, through Glasgow and its satellite towns in the centre, to the remote, mountainous parts of Lorne, the lovely Kintyre peninsula, and the southernmost islands of the Inner Hebrides. Within this area there is a fantastic variety of scenery and just on the mainland the tourist has the choice of a multitude of exciting itineraries. He may like to make for the delightful little loch-side town of Inveraray, with its famous castle, home of the Duke of Argyll (and recently badly damaged by fire). Inveraray is on Loch Fyne, and from here two routes are possible: one follows the northern shore of the Loch to reach the Kintyre peninsula, the other strikes northwards towards Loch Awe and some of the grandest scenery of the Western Highlands. The Kintyre peninsula is almost severed from the mainland at Tarbert; from here it is another forty-three miles to the southernmost tip of the peninsula, and from this point the Antrim coast of Northern Ireland is only twelve miles distant. Oban is a thriving resort as well as a busy rail and ferry terminus mainly dealing with traffic to and from Mull and other Hebridean islands. Iona, at the southern end of Mull, is famous as the birthplace of Christianity in Scotland. The Isle of Arran lies on the Firth of Clyde side of Kintyre and presents a microcosm of Highland beauty.

La région de Strathclyde comprend une grande partie du centre de l'Ecosse, partant de l'estuaire de la Clyde au sud, en passant par Glasgow et ses villes satellites, jusqu'aux lointaines montagnes d'Argyll, aux petites Hébrides et à la péninsule de Kintyre.

Die Gegend von Strathclyde umfaßt ein weites Gebiet in Mittelschottland, von den Badeorten am Forth of Clyde im Süden bis zu den abgelegenen Bergen von Argyll, den Inseln der Inneren Hebriden und der einsamen Kintyre-Halbinsel.

INVERARAY CASTLE, STRATHCLYDE

TARBERT ON THE KINTYRE PENINSULA

HOLY ISLAND FROM THE ISLE OF ARRAN

LOCH AWE AND KILCHURN CASTLE
OBAN, STRATHCLYDE

The Outer Hebrides, or Western Isles, off the west coast of Scotland, often cast a spell of magic on a visitor; invariably after an initial visit he will return again and again to savour their beauty and the unhurried way of life, so closely tied to the elements, of the inhabitants. The Outer Isles extend from the small, southernmost island of Barra to the Uists and the larger islands of Harris and Lewis in the north. Additional to these islands are the countless smaller ones offshore so that when one climbs to the summit of a mountain such as Heaval (on Barra) a wonderful array of islands stretches to the horizon. Yet all of the major islands have distinct characteristics: Barra, a mainly Catholic island, is small (eight miles by four) but has enough scenic beauty to last the visitor willing to explore it on a bicycle at least a fortnight. North and South Uist (with the island of Benbecula in between) are now linked by causeways. South Uist has a range of hills that are almost mountains, cut into by long sea lochs, while Benbecula and North Uist are much more flat, the landscape scattered with numerous lochans teeming with trout. The beaches are of unblemished, dazzling sand, and even on a summer's day will remain undisturbed apart from wandering sheep. Harris and Lewis are larger, the former having the more spectacular scenery of mountains and lochs. Much of the interior of Lewis is waterlogged peat-bog, but the coasts have a wild and lonely splendour.

Les grandes Hébrides, au large de la côte ouest de l'Ecosse, comprennent la minuscule île de Barra au sud, les îles d'Uist au milieu et les plus grandes îles d'Harris et Lewis au nord. Les liaisons aériennes et maritimes avec le reste du pays sont excellentes.

Die Außeren Hebriden sind eine Inselgruppe vor der Westküste Schottlands und setzt sich zusammen aus Barra, North und South Uist und schließlich Harris und Lewis. Die Flug- und Fährverbindungen mit dem Festland sind ausgezeichnet.

TIUMPHAN HEAD LIGHTHOUSE NEAR STORNAWAY, ISLE OF LEWIS

AN OLD 'BLACK HOUSE' AT ARDHASIG, NORTH HARRIS
LOCHMADDY HARBOUR, NORTH UIST

EAST KILBRIDE, SOUTH UIST

THE STATUE OF THE VIRGIN AND CHILD, HEAVAL, BARRA
SALTINISH, BARRA

LOCH LEVEN
FORT WILLIAM

URQUHART CASTLE ON LOCH NESS

LOCH NESS

INVERNESS CASTLE

The Great Glen runs diagonally across northern Scotland from Inverness in the east to Fort William in the south (both towns make excellent bases for exploring the Western Highlands). It was formed by a vast upheaval of two land masses, one against the other, the Great Glen being the natural indentation that follows the line of this geological fault. A series of beautiful lochs, dwarfed by great heights including Ben Nevis himself (at 4,406 feet the highest British summit), occupy the glen. The most famous of these is Loch Ness which is twenty-four miles long and has a maximum depth of more than 700 feet. It is in these murky underwater canyons that the monster is said to lurk. St Columba is reputed to have first seen the monster in the seventh century; since then there have been many sightings so that now the loch is under constant surveillance and ultra-modern equipment is used to identify underwater objects. Urquhart Castle is a favourite location for following this pursuit. Its romantic ruins overlook the length of the loch from a promontory on its northern shore. Its strategic importance accounted for its violent history (in the time of Robert the Bruce it changed hands four times in twelve years) so that it was already in ruins at the time of the 1715 Rising. Quite large boats can avoid the voyage around the top of Scotland by sailing through Loch Ness and to the west coast by the Caledonian Canal, a major feat of engineering which includes twenty-nine locks.

« Great Glen » est une faille géologique qui traverse le nord de l'Ecosse en diagonale, d'Inverness à Fort William. Une suite de « lochs » (lacs) magnifiques se trouve au creux de cette faille, dont le Loch Ness, célèbre pour son monstre.

Das „Great Glen" ist die geologische Verschiebung, die quer durch Schottland verläuft, von Inverness bis Fort William im Westen. Eine Reihe von Seen liegt in dem Glen, einschließlich des durch sein Seeungeheuer berühmten Loch Ness.

◀ EILEAN DONAN CASTLE

BRACADALE, LOCH HARPORT, AND THE CUILLINS, ISLE OF SKYE
ORD AND LOCH EICHART, ISLE OF SKYE

'The Road to the Isles'— the historic road that follows the northern shore of Loch Ness to cross the Highland massif by way of Glen Moriston and Glen Shiel — shows Highland scenery of imposing majesty. It leads under the steep flanks of mountains such as the Five Sisters and follows the shores of remote mountain and sea lochs. Eilean Donan Castle stands on a headland overlooking the meeting-point of three sea lochs. Possibly the most dramatically situated of all Highland castles, this stronghold of the Mackenzies was taken by the English after sea bombardment during the 1719 Rising and left in ruins. However in 1932 the castle was restored and it is now open to the public. The Road to the Isles ends at the Kyle of Lochalsh which was once a port busy with traffic from all of the Western Isles (as well as being the railhead), though now its importance depends on the short ferry link with Skye. The 'winged isle' (so called from its shape on the map) retains a separate identity even though only a mile or so of water divides it from the mainland. Much Gaelic is spoken on the island, especially in the more remote parts. The scenery is spectacular, with the Cuillins providing some of the best rock climbing to be found in Britain. Snug, white-washed crofts huddle beneath the steep slopes of the mountains, the crofters scraping a living from the sheep and cattle. Many people flee from the cares of the mainland to try to make an idyllic living here: some succeed, more return to the cities.

La « route des îles » est la route spectaculaire qui conduit d'Inverness à Kyle of Lochalsh sur la côte ouest, où un bac relie la côte à la belle île de Skye, endroit plein de magie où l'on parle le Gaélique aussi bien que l'Anglais.

,,The Road to the Isles'' ist eine eindrucksvolle Autostraße von Inverness zur Westküste bei Kyle of Lochalsh, wo eine Autofähre das Festland mit der schönen Insel Skye verbindet, einer zauberhaften Gegend, wo neben Englisch noch Gälisch gesprochen wird.

◀ ST MAGNUS'S CATHEDRAL

Scotland's offshore islands are so diverse that to visit any of them from the mainland is usually to discover a different country. Certainly this is true of the Orkney Islands, situated about twenty miles off the north coast. Here the atmosphere left by the frequent invasions of Vikings many centuries ago still lingers. The land is green and fertile, though as in the Western Isles high winds prevent trees from flourishing. The beaches are of fine silver sand, the daylight lasts almost until midnight in the summer, and there is a wealth of prehistoric sites to explore: these are three ingredients that explain the islands' success as holiday haunts and there are many more. Of the sixty-seven islands within the Orkney group, twenty-one are inhabited. Kirkwall is the capital of the largest group of three islands, the two southern islands being linked to the 'mainland' by causeways built by Italian prisoners of war to protect the naval anchorage of Scapa Flow (after a German submarine had sunk the British battleship *Royal Oak* at anchor early in the Second World War). The cathedral at Kirkwall, dedicated to St Magnus, is of a size and beauty that surpass many more famous cathedrals in Scotland or England. It dates from 1137 and masons from Durham probably worked here, putting up massive pillars to support the nave vaulting that shows Norman-style work at its most impressive. The cathedral is unique in that it belongs to the town of Kirkwall rather than to any specific ecclesiastical body.

Les îles Orkney sont situées à environ 30 kilomètres au nord de la côte écossaise. Sur soixante-sept îles, vingt et une sont habitées. De nombreux visiteurs ont été surpris par la grandeur de la cathédrale Normande St Magnus à Kirkwall.

Die Orkneys liegen 32 km nördlich des schottischen Festlands. Die Inselgruppe setzt sich zusammen aus 67 Inseln, von denen 21 bewohnt sind. Die normannische St.-Magnus-Kathedrale beeindruckt viele Besucher durch ihre Erhabenheit.

KWALL, ORKNEY ISLANDS
STROMNESS HARBOUR, ORKNEY ISLANDS
KITCHENER MONUMENT, MARWICK HEAD, ORKNEY ISLANDS

CAPE WRATH, SUTHERLAND, HIGHLAND REGION

THE CAIRNGORMS FROM NEAR DULNAIN BRIDGE

PINE-FRINGED LOCH MORLICH

THE RIVER SPEY

Scotland's eastern massif — the Grampian chain of mountains — covers much of the centre and east of the country. For the most part the Grampians are lonely, heather-covered hills, though parts of them are thrust up higher to form mountain ranges in their own right. The Cairngorm range is one of these: essentially it is a tableland which has several peaks topping the 4,000-foot mark (these are called 'munros' locally). These mountains enjoy a dual, seasonal, popularity. In summer walkers, climbers, and even dinghy sailors enjoy the amenities of the area (dinghies sail on Loch Morlich, with its lovely fringe of pines; it is more than a thousand feet above sea level). An excellent road leads up to the chair-lift which is operated all during summer and winter months. In winter skiers converge on the flourishing resorts that were quiet villages until a few years ago to make use of Britain's best ski slopes. Facilities here are claimed to be better than at many continental resorts and snow is usually plentiful. The area is also famous for its salmon rivers, the Spey being particularly outstanding. Grantown-on-Spey makes a good centre for exploring these eastern highlands. The village was planned by Sir James Grant in the eighteenth century to an elegant, spacious design. In Victorian times its prosperity was assured when doctors prescribed a stay in Grantown, with its fresh mountain air, as a remedy for a variety of ills. Perhaps the products of nearby distilleries also helped!

THE SKI-LIFT NEAR AVIEMORE
LOCH GARTEN

Les meilleures pistes de ski d'Ecosse se trouvent dans les Cairngorms, à l'est du pays. Grantown-on-Spey ou Aviemore offrent des services qui peuvent rivaliser avec ceux d'autres stations européennes et après Noël la neige y est en général abondante.

Die Bergkette der Cairngorms bietet viele der besten Skihänge im Lande. Die Wintersporteinrichtungen in Aviemore oder Grantown-on-Spey können sich mit denen kontinentaler Wintersportorte messen, und nach Weihnachten gibt es meist viel Schnee.

BURGHEAD HARBOUR, GRAMPIAN
THE OLD BRIDGE OF DEE, BRAEMAR ▶

ABERDEEN
BALMORAL CASTLE

Aberdeen is Scotland's third largest city, and possibly the wealthiest since the offshore oilfields have revived its fortunes so dramatically. The older buildings of the city are of the famous local pink granite which also features in many famous edifices much further afield. Aberdeen's prosperity was formerly based on its fishing fleet, but this has declined in numbers as the herring left the waters of the North Sea (though many bigger boats sail for deep-sea fishing grounds from Aberdeen). The River Dee meets the sea here. Royal Deeside gets its name from the Queen's country home in Scotland — Balmoral Castle. In 1852 Prince Albert engaged William Smith, city architect of Aberdeen, to supply designs for the baronial-styled castle that we see today. It was a favourite holiday home of Queen Victoria even after the death of her husband, and she wrote of it as 'this dear paradise'. The setting of the castle amidst fragrant pine woods is certainly magnificent, and the grounds are open to the public in early summer when the Queen is not in residence. Braemar, about seven miles to the west of Balmoral, also has royal connections. Its fame as a hunting resort brought royalty and nobility to its deer forests as early as the seventeenth century, and the Jacobite revolt of 1715 sprang from a 'hunt' held here by the Earl of Mar at which the standard was raised for King James VIII. The first Braemar Gathering was held in 1832 and this annual September event remains a red-letter day for the Highlanders.

Le château de Balmoral est la résidence écossaise de la Reine. Il est situé à environ quatre-vingt kilomètres à l'ouest d'Aberdeen. Balmoral jouit d'un site splendide sur le Dee, au milieu de forêts de pins et d'une magnifique chaîne de montagnes.

Die schottische Residenz der Königin ist Balmoral Castle, ungefähr 80 km westlich von Aberdeen, der drittgrößten Stadt Schottlands. Balmoral liegt wunderschön am Fluß Dee inmitten duftender Tannenforste und eindrucksvoller Berge.

◀ LOCH TUMMEL, TAYSIDE

THE RIVER TAY, PERTH
CRAIL, FIFE

Perth — 'the fair city' — has traditionally been one of the gateways to the Highlands. Its beautiful position on the west bank of the River Tay is best seen from Kinnoull Hill, a vantage-point to the east of the city which also gives a splendid view down the river to the Firth of Tay and the hills of Fife. Crail is one of the loveliest of Scottish fishing villages. The old red-tiled, crow-stepped houses overlooking the harbour have been carefully restored by the National Trust for Scotland, and then resold to people who enjoy living in homes full of character and history. Crail has had a chequered history, having been a busy port until the seventeenth century when a decline in trade, made worse by a severe outbreak of plague, saw its fortunes at a low ebb. Smuggling was a favourite pastime in later centuries, but this activity ended when Crail became a popular holiday resort with the gentry of Edinburgh and its prosperity increased. St Andrews is about ten miles north-west of Crail. Golfing enthusiasts venerate its Royal and Ancient as the mecca of all golf clubs, but besides this the town claims attention as having the oldest university in the country, founded in 1422, and the beautiful ruins of a cathedral which was once the focus of religious life in Scotland. The ruins of the castle, also of historical importance, for John Knox was captured here by the French, stand on the cliffs overlooking the bay. The Martyrs' Monument nearby commemorates the reformers burnt in the town for their faith.

On appelle Perth la « Belle Ville » (The Fair City), et il est vrai que son site sur les rives de la Tay est magnifique. Crail est un village de pêcheurs sur la côte de Fife, et possède un port charmant surplombé de maisons soigneusement restaurées.

Perth ist bekannt als die „Fair City", und die Lage an den Ufern des Flusses Tay ist zweifellos entzückend. Crail ist eine Fischerdorf an der Küste von Fife mit einem bezaubernden Hafen, den alte, geschickt renovierte Häuser überblicken.

LOCH LUBNAIG, CENTRAL REGION

LOCH ARD, CENTRAL REGION
LOCH ACHRAY, TROSSACHS

LOCH LOMOND

LOCH KATRINE, TROSSACHS
THE TROSSACHS HOTEL, LOCH ACHRAY

Sir Walter Scott was the first publicist for the lovely Trossachs region of Central Scotland, for he used it for the setting of his poem *Lady of the Lake* and for many incidents in his epic telling of the story of Rob Roy. Trossachs takes its name from a word meaning 'bristly country' and is really only correct when it refers to the wooded valley between Lochs Achray and Katrine, though geographical licence is often taken to take in much of the surrounding countryside. Scott wrote of these remote parts in the days when travellers would find it difficult, if not impossible, to reach them. However, soon afterwards the area became an accepted part of the Grand Tour of the Romantics when William Wordsworth visited, and wrote about, its wonders. Loch Lomond, to the west of the Trossachs, has long been celebrated in song, verse and evocative prose. Its situation so close to the boundaries of Glasgow has inevitably led to some commercialisation of its lower reaches, but as the traveller progresses northwards the influence of man shows less and less and we are left with indelible impressions of wooded shores and overtowering mountains. A road follows Loch Lomond's western shore throughout its twenty-four-mile length, but it is always best to leave the car to appreciate the beautiful scenery from one of the many signposted viewpoints that overlook the thirty or so wooded islands scattered about the loch and the imposing shape of Ben Lomond (3,129 feet) beyond.

La région des Trossachs est une très belle région du centre de l'Ecosse située autour du Loch Achray, et rendue célèbre par le poème de Sir Walter Scott *Lady of the Lake*. Le Loch Lomond a aussi été vanté par des poèmes et des chansons.

Die Trossachs ist eine liebliche Gegend in Mittelschottland um Loch Achray, den Sir Walter Scott durch sein Gedicht *Lady of the Lake* berühmt machte. Loch Lomond ist 40 km lang, und seine Schönheit wird in Gedichten und Liedern gerühmt.

EDINBURGH CASTLE

WHITE HORSE CLOSE

As befits a capital city, Edinburgh is a place of immense beauty and memorable character. It is a city of two faces: the old part spreads around the castle in a tangle of narrow streets and enclosed wynds, consisting of the tall buildings so characteristic of the city — the earliest skyscrapers! The main thoroughfare of the Old Town (Canongate and High Street) is also known as the Royal Mile since it was the route of kings travelling between Holyrood Palace and the castle. The New Town is to the north of Princes Street Gardens (which occupy the site of the Nor' Loch, drained in the early eighteenth century). Wide roads, built to a pattern of blocks, are lined by terraces of handsome Georgian houses: the New Town was one of the earliest exercises in town planning in Britain. The castle is dominant over both parts of the city. It was built by Edwin, King of Northumbria, who gave his name to the city by putting up the first stronghold on the steep volcanic rock in the seventh century. Nothing remains of this structure, the oldest part of the present castle being the chapel built by Queen Margaret on the highest part of the rock in 1076. The Royal Apartments date from the sixteenth century and visitors. are shown the tiny room where Mary, Queen of Scots gave birth to the young prince who was to become James VI of Scotland, James I of England. Those visiting the city for the first time may be startled by the gun fired from the battlements of the castle each day at one o'clock.

Edimbourg, la ville aux sept collines avec la mer à ses pieds, possède aussi un château romantique au centre, construit sur un rocher escarpé. C'est l'une des plus belles capitales du monde et son Festival attire des milliers de visiteurs chaque année.

Edinburgh, eine Stadt auf sieben Hügeln mit der See zu ihren Füßen, hat auch eine romantische Burg auf einer steilen Felsklippe in der Stadtmitte. Es ist eine der schönsten Hauptstädte der Welt, und das alljährliche Festival lockt viele Besuchern an.

THE SEARCHLIGHT TATTOO – CLIMAX OF THE EDINBURGH FESTIVAL

85306 716 3
© Copyright 1977 Jarrold & Sons Ltd, Norwich
Published and printed in Great Britain by
Jarrold & Sons Ltd, Norwich   277

BACK COVER: THE MAJESTIC MOUNTAIN SCENERY OF GLEN COE